SHOW TIME!

Familiar Tales
for Little Actors

Adapted by Diane Head

Good Apple

Editor: Susan Eddy

Designer: April Okano

Cover Illustration: Judith Moffatt

Good Apple
An Imprint of Modern Curriculum
A Division of Simon & Schuster
299 Jefferson Road, P.O. Box 480
Parsippany, NJ 07054-0480

ISBN 1-56417-680-0

1 2 3 4 5 6 7 8 9 BB 01 00 99 98 97

CONTENTS

Jack and the Beanstalk. . . 6

∎

Goldilocks and the Three Bears. . . 20

∎

The Little Red Hen. . . 27

∎

The Gingerbread Man. . . 34

∎

The Three Little Pigs. . . 43

∎

Chicken Licken. . . 54

∎

The Three Billy Goats Gruff. . . 62

∎

Hansel and Gretel. . . 72

∎

The Bremen Town Musicians. . . 84

∎

Little Red Riding Hood. . . 92

∎

Cinderella. . . 100

∎

INTRODUCTION

What better way to introduce young readers to the world of literature and the performing arts than through drama? *Show Time!* contains scripts of eleven well-known stories for children just beginning their reading journey. The plays are perfect for kindergartners, first graders, some second graders, and Title One readers. The fairy tale scripts have been adapted for four to six children and one proficient reader—a teacher, parent, or older student—who acts as the narrator.

The scripts are simply written and repetitive in nature, so there is little need to preteach vocabulary. At the beginning of each script is a word list that can serve as

an easily-scanned reference for placing children in suitable plays. Each play can be performed as reader's theater, puppet theater, or as an actual live performance, depending on the teacher's purposes and the children's skills.

Stage directions have not been included, as they would be inappropriate for the children's reading levels. Invite children to discuss and decide such things as tone of voice and movement on stage for the characters in the plays. The main idea is for you and your emergent readers to have fun reading and performing.

JACK AND THE BEANSTALK

WORD LIST

a	fum	little	some
about	get	look	sorry
again	giant's	mad	supper
am	give	me	take
any	go	mean	talking
be	gold	meat	tell
beans	good	money	thank
beanstalk	harp	more	that
been	have	mother	that's
big	he'll	must	the
but	hello	my	there
cake	help	need	this
caught	hen	no	to
climb	her	not	trouble
come	here	OK	tum
cool	hide	our	up
cow	his	pet	want
did	hope	right	was
does	house	room	wasn't
don't	how	run	we
egg	hurry	said	what
faster	I	salad	where
fee	in	secret	who
fi	is	sell	why
fill	it	she	will
fo	Jack	show	wow
food	Jack's	smart	yes
for	just	smell	you
from	know	so	your

JACK AND THE BEANSTALK

CHARACTERS

Narrator
Jack
Mother
Beanstalk
Giant
Giant's Wife

PROPS

paper beanstalk
several beans
gold-foil wrapped coins
plate
egg
hen (stuffed or cut
from cardboard)
cardboard harp

Narrator: Once upon a time in a rather magical place, there lived a young man named Jack and his mother.

Jack: I am Jack.

Mother: I am Jack's mother.

Narrator: They lived quite simply in a run-down cottage. They barely had enough food to get by. So one day, Jack's mother decided that they had to sell their pet cow because she no longer gave milk and she ate too much.

Mother: Take the cow. Sell her.

Jack: But she is our pet.

Mother: I am sorry.

Narrator: Jack cried, argued, and even tried a good old-fashioned temper tantrum, but his mother did not change her mind.

Mother: Sell the cow.

Jack: OK.

Narrator: Sadly Jack led the pet cow to the market. There he met an old man who was lonely enough to buy the unusual pet. Unfortunately he had only magic beans to give Jack for the cow. Being a simple sort of fellow, Jack took the beans and went home.

Jack: Mother! Look what I have!

Mother: What?

Jack: Beans!

Mother: Beans? We need money, not beans!

Jack: Money?

Mother: Money! Go to your room! No supper!

Narrator: Jack's mother didn't even think of cooking the beans for supper. If she had, the story would have turned out very differently. Instead she tossed them out the window.

Mother: There!

Narrator: Jack's mother went to bed without her supper, too. But during the night, a fantastic thing happened. The beans sprouted and grew into a mighty magical beanstalk that reached high into the clouds. When Jack and his mother got up the next morning, they were amazed.

Jack: Wow!

Mother: What is that?

Narrator: Jack, having done all the gardening for his mother, knew a beanstalk when he saw one.

Jack: It is a beanstalk.

Mother: How did it get so big?

Narrator: Jack shrugged his shoulders. Being a curious sort of fellow, he reached out his hand and touched the beanstalk.

Beanstalk: Hello.

Jack: Who said that?

Mother: It wasn't me!

Beanstalk: It was me ... the beanstalk.

Jack: A talking beanstalk?

©1997 Good Apple

Beanstalk: That's right.

Narrator: Jack and his mother were blown away. They had never heard of such a thing as a talking beanstalk.

Beanstalk: I know a secret.

Jack: Will you tell me?

Beanstalk: I will show you. Climb up.

Narrator: Jack just had to know what the secret was so he did as the beanstalk asked. He climbed up and up and up until his house was just a tiny dot and his head was in the clouds.

Beanstalk: Just a little more.

Jack: OK.

Narrator: When Jack's head poked through the clouds, he couldn't believe his eyes! There on top of the clouds was a golden mansion!

Beanstalk: Go in.

Narrator: Jack was a bit scared to step on a cloud, having learned all about them in science class. But the beanstalk seemed a trustworthy sort, so Jack let go of the beanstalk and stepped onto a cloud.

Jack: Wow! This is cool.

Beanstalk: Go in.

Jack: You mean … in the house?

Beanstalk: Yes.

Narrator: Outside the mansion a gigantic woman was arranging puffs of clouds into sculptures. Jack snuck by her and went in.

Jack: Wow! This is cool.

Beanstalk: Take some.

Jack: Some what?

Beanstalk: Some gold.

Narrator: Sure enough, there on the table was a pile of gold. Just as he was about to stuff a handful into his pocket, Jack heard a terrible noise.

Beanstalk: Hide!

Narrator: Jack hid behind a stack of gold coins.

Giant: Fee fi fo fum! Get me food to fill my tum!

Narrator: It was the giant! The giant's wife rushed in.

Giant's Wife: Here is food.

Narrator: The giant's wife plunked down a huge platter of carrots and celery.

©1997 Good Apple

Giant: I want meat.

Giant's Wife: We don't have any.

Giant: I smell meat.

Narrator: The giant's wife scratched her head. She looked everywhere in the refrigerator for meat. She took so long that the giant fell asleep at the table. Jack knew that this was his chance to escape. He filled his pockets with gold and ran out of the giant's house as fast as he could.

Beanstalk: Hurry!

Jack: He'll be mad about his gold.

Beanstalk: Yes.

Narrator: Jack had been taught not to steal. He hesitated and looked back at the mansion. Maybe he should return the coins. Just then, he heard the giant roar!

Giant: Where is my gold?

Narrator: Jack slid down the beanstalk without a second thought. He frowned at the beanstalk.

Jack: You will get me in trouble.

Narrator: The beanstalk didn't answer.

Jack: Mother!

Mother: Where have you been?

Jack: I have been to the giant's house. Look!

Narrator: Jack turned his pockets inside out. The gold fell to the ground.

Mother: Where did you get it?

Jack: From the giant.

Mother: Does he know?

Jack: Yes.

Mother: He will get you.

Jack: I hope not.

Narrator: Jack and his mother were happy for a while, and Jack and the beanstalk became good friends. But one day, all the gold coins had been spent. Jack told his sad tale to the beanstalk.

Jack: We have no money.

Beanstalk: Climb up.

Jack: Not again.

Beanstalk: Why not?

Jack: I will get caught.

©1997 Good Apple

Beanstalk: No, you won't.

Narrator: Jack should have been a bit older and a bit wiser by now. Jack knew better, but up he climbed anyway. Again, the golden mansion was just above the white clouds.

Beanstalk: Go in.

Narrator: Jack was scared. He knew that the giant had to be around somewhere.

Beanstalk: Go in.

Narrator: Jack snuck into the giant's house. Inside, the giant's wife was making a cake. She was too busy to notice a little creature like Jack.

Giant's Wife: This cake will be good.

Narrator: Jack spied a speckled hen in the corner. It cackled and laid a golden egg. Jack could hardly believe his eyes.

Giant's Wife: Thank you for the egg, hen.

Narrator: The giant's wife picked up the egg and put it in a basket with more golden eggs. Now, Jack had been taught better manners, but he thought maybe he would just borrow the hen for a few days. So he grabbed the hen, carefully holding her beak shut. Suddenly he heard the giant's footsteps.

Giant: Fee, fi, fo, fum!

Giant's Wife: Here is a cake!

Giant: I want meat!

Giant's Wife: We don't have any meat.

Giant: I smell meat!

Narrator: The giant's wife scratched her head and looked in the cupboards for meat. She took so long that the giant fell asleep in his chair and Jack was able to escape from the house with the hen.

Beanstalk: Hurry!

Jack: He'll be mad about the hen.

Beanstalk: Yes.

Narrator: Just as Jack was descending the beanstalk, the hen gave a squawk. The giant awoke and roared!

Giant: Where is my hen?

Narrator: Jack slid down the beanstalk so fast that he got beanstalk burns on his hands. He frowned at the beanstalk.

Jack: You will get me in trouble.

Narrator: The beanstalk didn't answer.

Jack: Mother!

Mother: Where have you been?

Jack: I have been to the giant's house. Look!

Narrator: Jack showed his mother the hen, and the hen laid another golden egg.

Mother: Is it the giant's hen?

Jack: Yes.

Mother: He will get you.

Jack: I hope not.

Narrator: And so Jack and his mother were happy for a while, until the naughty beanstalk stirred up trouble again.

Beanstalk: Jack.

Jack: What?

Beanstalk: Climb up.

Jack: Not again.

Beanstalk: Why not?

Jack: I will get caught.

Beanstalk: No, you won't.

©1997 Good Apple

Jack: OK. But this is the last time.

Narrator: So up Jack climbed for a third time. He really wasn't surprised to see the giant's house on top of the clouds, but he was scared.

Beanstalk: Go in.

Jack: This is not smart.

Narrator: But since he'd come this far, Jack thought he had nothing to lose. He tiptoed into the giant's house. The giant's wife was tossing a salad, and the giant was nowhere in sight.

Giant's Wife: This salad will be good.

Narrator: Jack saw a beautiful golden harp against the wall. Maybe he'd just borrow it. His mother loved music. He picked it up.

Giant: Fee, fi, fo, fum!

Giant's Wife: Here is a salad.

Giant: I want meat!

Giant's Wife: We don't have any meat.

Giant: But I smell meat.

©1997 Good Apple

Narrator: Jack saw the giant himself begin to sniff around. Trembling, Jack sprinted for the door. The harp's strings vibrated in the breeze, and the giant spotted Jack.

Giant: I *did* smell meat!

Jack: Help!

Beanstalk: Run!

Narrator: Jack ran very fast, but the giant's legs were much, much longer. Just as the giant reached way down to get him, Jack reached the beanstalk.

Beanstalk: Hurry!

Jack: Help! He is mad about the harp!

Beanstalk: Yes!

Giant: My harp! Give me my harp!

Narrator: Jack slid down the beanstalk. Leaves flew everywhere as his feet sheared them off. That, of course, left very little for the giant to hold on to.

Jack: Help!

Giant: Help!

Beanstalk: Faster, Jack!

Narrator: Jack reached the ground just in time to escape being crushed by the giant. The giant hit the ground so hard that he caused an earthquake, which promptly swallowed him up along with the naughty beanstalk. Jack and his mother bought back their pet cow and lived happily ever after with the cow, the hen, and the harp. And Jack never again felt tempted to borrow from a giant, and he never, never, ever planted another bean plant for as long as he lived.

GOLDILOCKS AND THE THREE BEARS

a	eaten	it's	sitting
all	fine	just	sleep
an	for	let's	sleeping
and	go	mama	soft
baby	Goldilocks	me	someone
bear	gone	mine	there
bed	hard	much	this
been	has	my	tired
big	have	one	to
broken	help	papa	too
call	her	police	walk
called	here	porridge	want
can	home	right	where
chair	hot	scare	with
cold	hungry	scared	yes
did	I	she	you
didn't	I'm	should	
door	in	shut	
eat	is	sit	

©1997 Good Apple

GOLDILOCKS AND THE THREE BEARS

CHARACTERS	PROPS
Narrator	three bowls
Papa Bear	three spoons
Mama Bear	three chairs
Baby Bear	three "beds"
Goldilocks	

Narrator: Once upon a time, a family of grizzly bears lived in a charming little cottage in the forest.

Papa Bear: I am Papa Bear.

Mama Bear: I am Mama Bear.

Baby Bear: And I am Baby Bear.

Narrator: Because the bears were always so busy in the forest, their chores, such as cooking, cleaning, and making the beds, were often done sloppily. One day, Mama Bear served porridge for breakfast.

Papa Bear: Mine is too hot.

Mama Bear: Mine is too cold.

Baby Bear: Mine is just right.

Narrator: Baby Bear was not allowed to eat his porridge, even if it was just right, because it would be rude to eat when no one else could. So instead of solving the problem in a creative way, the bears went for a walk in the forest.

Papa Bear: Let's go for a walk.

Mama Bear: Fine with me.

Baby Bear: I want to eat!

Narrator: No sooner had they left the cottage, then along came a very snoopy little girl named Goldilocks.

Goldilocks: I am Goldilocks.

Narrator: Although Goldilocks knew better, when she saw the charming little cottage, she couldn't help herself, and she went in. There on the table was the bears' porridge.

Goldilocks: Porridge!

Narrator: After her long walk, Goldilocks was hungry. She ate not only Papa Bear's porridge, but Mama Bear's and Baby Bear's, too.

Goldilocks: This one is too hot.
This one is too cold.
This one is just right!

Narrator: And she ate every bit. Now, eating all that porridge made Goldilocks feel lazy, so she searched for a chair.

Goldilocks: Where can I sit?

Narrator: Goldilocks found three chairs—a very large one, a not-so-large one, and a little bitty one. She just had to try each one.

Goldilocks: This one is much too big.
This one is too big, too.
This one is just right!

Narrator: But sleeping in a chair isn't comfortable at all, as Goldilocks soon found out. She squirmed so much that the little chair broke and dumped her on the floor. Bruised and aching, Goldilocks looked for a bed.

Goldilocks: Where can I sleep?

Narrator: Goldilocks found three beds—a very large one, a not-so-large one, and a little bitty one. She tried out each of them.

Goldilocks: This one is too hard.
This one is too soft.
This one is just right!

©1997 Good Apple

Narrator: And soon Goldilocks was fast asleep and snoring away. Meanwhile, the bears were tired of walking in the forest and decided to go home.

Papa Bear: I am hungry.

Mama Bear: I am tired.

Baby Bear: I want to go home!

Narrator: The bears were surprised to find the front door open when they arrived home.

Papa Bear: Didn't you shut the door?

Mama Bear: Yes, I did.

Baby Bear: Call the police!

Narrator: Baby Bear had a good idea, but his parents didn't call the police. Instead they went inside.

Papa Bear: Someone has been here.

Mama Bear: Someone has.

Baby Bear: I'm scared!

Narrator: The first thing they saw was the table with the empty porridge bowls.

Papa Bear: Someone has eaten my porridge.

Mama Bear: Someone has eaten *my* porridge.

Baby Bear: Someone has eaten *my* porridge. It's all gone!

Narrator: And Baby Bear began to cry. Mama Bear fixed Baby Bear a quick peanut butter and honey sandwich. Tired after their long walk, they went to sit in their chairs.

Papa Bear: Someone has been sitting in my chair.

Mama Bear: Someone has been sitting in *my* chair.

Baby Bear: Someone has been sitting in *my* chair, and it's broken!

Narrator: Baby Bear began crying again. Mama Bear dried his tears and found a tube of epoxy glue. She glued the broken chair back together. All in all, it hadn't been a very good day, so the bears decided to go to bed. Boy, were they surprised at what they found!

Papa Bear: Someone has been sleeping in my bed.

Mama Bear: Someone has been sleeping in *my* bed.

Baby Bear: Someone has been sleeping in *my* bed, and there she is!

Narrator: The bears whispered among themselves while Goldilocks snored away. What should they do?

Papa Bear: Let's eat her!

Mama Bear: Let's scare her!

Baby Bear: Let's call the police!

Narrator: The discussion became an argument— a loud one.

Papa Bear: Eat her!

Mama Bear: Scare her!

Baby Bear: Call the police!

Narrator: The ruckus woke Goldilocks. She leapt out of bed, screaming for help.

Goldilocks: Help! Help!

Narrator: The three bears were so startled that they just stood there and stared as Goldilocks ran from their cottage and vanished in the forest.

Papa Bear: We should have eaten her.

Mama Bear: We should have scared her.

Baby Bear: We should have called the police.

Narrator: The three bears never did decide what would have been the best thing to do, but it really didn't matter because they never saw Goldilocks again. And they all lived happily ever after.

THE LITTLE RED HEN

WORD LIST

a	go	nap	TV
am	good	no	was
and	hard	not	watch
bread	have	pig	we
can	help	plant	will
cards	hen	play	work
cat	her	red	you
corn	I	seeds	
did	it	smells	
dog	keep	soon	
eat	let's	swim	
fishing	little	take	
for	looks	that	
friend	me	the	

THE LITTLE RED HEN

CHARACTERS	PROPS
Narrator	purse
Little Red Hen	three pillows
Dog	deck of cards
Cat	hoe
Pig	three fishing poles
	loaf pan
	three towels
	package of seeds
	watering can

Narrator: Once upon a time, there was a little red hen who lived on a farm with her friends—a dog, a cat, and a pig.

Little Red Hen: I am the little red hen.

Dog: I am her friend the dog.

Cat: I am her friend the cat.

Pig: And I am her friend the pig.

Narrator: One day, the little red hen got very hungry for some fresh corn bread. She looked in the refrigerator, but there was none. She looked in the cupboards, and even in the dishwasher.

Little Red Hen: No corn bread!

Narrator: What was she to do? The little red hen picked up her purse and set out for the market. There she bought a package of corn seeds.

Little Red Hen: I will plant the seeds. Soon I will have corn for corn bread.

Narrator: The little red hen went home, hoping that her three friends would help her get the soil ready.

Little Red Hen: Will you help me?

Dog: No, not I.

Cat: No, not I.

Pig: No, not I.

Dog: Let's take a nap.

Narrator: And so they did. The little red hen shook her head, got out her hoe, and worked hard getting the soil ready. Finally it was time to plant the seeds. She woke her three friends.

Little Red Hen: Will you help me?

Dog: No, not I.

Cat: No, not I.

Pig: No, not I.

Cat: Let's play cards.

Narrator: And so they did. The little red hen had no choice but to plant the corn seeds all by herself. She was very tired, and her back hurt by the time she was through, but her feathers weren't too badly ruffled. Yet.

Little Red Hen: That was hard work.

Dog: Not for me.

Cat: Not for me.

Pig: And not for me.

Narrator: Time passed, and soon the corn began to grow. The little red hen saw that it needed weeding and watering. She went to her friends for help.

Little Red Hen: Will you help me?

Dog: No, not I.

Cat: No, not I.

Pig: No, not I. Let's run and play.

Narrator: And so they did. The little red hen sighed and went to work all by herself. After tending the garden, she was all worn out.

Little Red Hen: That was hard work.

Dog: Not for me.

Cat: Not for me.

Pig: And not for me.

Narrator: More days passed, and the corn grew tall. It was time to pick the ears of corn, but the little red hen, being rather short, couldn't quite reach the ears. She needed help. She found her friends fishing in the stream.

Little Red Hen: Will you help me?

Dog: No, not I.

Cat: No, not I.

Pig: No, not I.

Dog: Let's keep fishing.

Narrator: The little red hen sighed. She would have to pick the corn all by herself. She found a ladder and went up and down, up and down all day long and well into the night until all the corn had been picked. Every muscle in her body ached.

Little Red Hen: That was hard work.

Dog: Not for me.

Cat: Not for me.

Pig: And not for me.

Narrator: The little red hen was becoming a bit vexed. Could there be a pattern developing, she wondered? She thought about the delicious corn bread she would make, and she knew she couldn't quit now. The next day, she would have to shuck the corn and grind it, so she went to her friends.

Little Red Hen: Will you help me?

Dog: No, not I.

Cat: No, not I.

Pig: No, not I.

Cat: Let's watch TV.

Narrator: And so they did. The little red hen did all the work by herself. Finally the corn was ground and ready to be made into corn bread.

Little Red Hen: That was hard work.

Dog: Not for me.

Cat: Not for me.

Pig: And not for me.

Narrator: By now, the little red hen could almost taste the delicious corn bread. Shrugging her shoulders, she collected the ingredients for corn bread, and set them all out. She asked again.

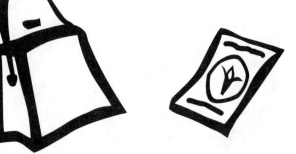

Little Red Hen: Will you help me?

Dog: No, not I.

Cat: No, not I.

Pig: No, not I. Let's go for a swim.

Narrator: And so they did, leaving the little red hen to do all the work again. She made a scrumptious pan of corn bread and set it on the table to cool. Just then, the three friends returned from their swim. They saw the corn bread and their stomachs growled.

Dog: It looks good.

Cat: It smells good.

Pig: May we eat it?

Narrator: The little red hen thought of all the hours she'd spent and all her sore muscles, and she lost her temper.

Little Red Hen: No, you may not! You did not help.

Narrator: Her friends began to cry, but the little red hen was not sorry for them. She sat down and gobbled up every crumb right in front of them. And when it was all gone, she packed her bags and went to live in another town where she found real chicken friends and she lived happily ever after.

THE GINGERBREAD MAN

WORD LIST

a	eat	man	too
across	fast	maybe	very
after	faster	me	wait
am	fox	melt	want
and	get	my	water
are	gingerbread	nose	we
as	goodbye	oh	wet
away	have	old	what
back	he	on	who
boy	head	onto	will
but	help	ran	woman
can	him	river	won't
can't	how	run	wow
catch	I	swim	yes
climb	I'm	than	you
cookies	is	that	yum
deep	it	the	
do	know	they	
don't	make	to	

THE GINGERBREAD MAN

CHARACTERS

Narrator
Old Man
Old Woman
Gingerbread Man
Boy
Girl
Fox

PROPS

cookies
paper river

Narrator: Once upon a time in a land far away, an old man became very hungry for gingerbread. Now, the old man's wife was an excellent cook, so she volunteered to make some gingerbread cookies.

Old Man: I want gingerbread cookies.

Old Woman: Me, too.

Narrator: That day, the old woman felt very creative, so after forming several dozen gingerbread cookies, she cleverly thought up a cookie shaped like a man.

Old Woman: I will make a gingerbread man.

Old Man: I will eat it! Yum!

Narrator: Soon the delicious aroma of gingerbread filled the house.

Old Man: I can't wait!

Old Woman: You have to.

Narrator: The old woman finally opened the oven. Much to her astonishment, out jumped a gingerbread man!

Gingerbread Man: I am the gingerbread man!

Old Woman: Oh my!

Old Man: Wow!

Narrator: The gingerbread man began to dance around the house. As determined as the old people were to eat him, the gingerbread man was just as determined *not* to be eaten. He jumped out of the old man's reach and sang:

Gingerbread Man: Run, run as fast as you can!
You can't catch me!
I'm the gingerbread man!

Narrator: And the gingerbread man took off running. The old man and the old woman laced up their Nikes and took off after him.

Old Man: Let's get him!

Old Woman: Run!

©1997 Good Apple

Narrator: The gingerbread man laughed as he ran past a little boy.

Boy: Who are you?

Gingerbread Man: I am the gingerbread man.

Boy: Gingerbread? Yum!

Gingerbread Man: I ran faster than the old man.
I ran faster than the old woman.
And I can run faster than you!

Narrator: The gingerbread man stuck out his tongue quite disrespectfully and sang:

Gingerbread Man: Run, run as fast as you can!
You can't catch me!
I'm the gingerbread man!

Narrator: The boy couldn't resist the challenge. He joined in the chase, with the old man and the old woman close behind.

Old Man: Let's get him!

Old Woman: Run!

Boy: He can't get away!

Narrator: The gingerbread man laughed so hard that it slowed him up a bit. He stopped to catch his breath. A girl walked by.

Girl: Who are you?

Gingerbread Man: I am the gingerbread man!

Girl: Gingerbread? Yum!

Gingerbread Man: Uh oh!

Girl: I will eat you!

Gingerbread Man: I ran faster than the old man.
I ran faster than the old woman.
I ran faster than the boy.
And I can run faster than you!

Narrator: The gingerbread man poked his gingerbread fingers in his gingerbread ears and waggled them as he sang:

Gingerbread Man: Run, run as fast as you can!
You can't catch me!
I'm the gingerbread man!

Narrator: Well, the girl wanted to eat the gingerbread man too, so off she went—with the boy, the old man, and the old woman close behind.

Old Man: Let's get him!

Old Woman: Run!

©1997 Good Apple

Boy: He can't get away!

Girl: Faster!

Narrator: The gingerbread man was having a fine time—the most fun, in fact, that he'd ever had in his whole life. He giggled and laughed so much that he had to stop to catch his breath.

Gingerbread Man: I am fast!

Narrator: The gingerbread man glanced over his gingerbread shoulder. The old man, the old woman, the boy, and the girl were running hard, but they were not as fast as he was.

Gingerbread Man: I am very fast!

Narrator: The gingerbread man looked ahead. His mouth dropped open when he saw what was in his path.

Gingerbread Man: What is that?

Narrator: From the bushes appeared a creature he'd never seen before.

Fox: I am the fox.

Gingerbread Man: Yes, but what is that?

Narrator: The fox looked in the direction the gingerbread man was pointing.

Fox: It is a river.

Gingerbread Man: What is that?

Fox: It is water.

Gingerbread Man: Water?

Fox: Yes, deep water.

Narrator: The gingerbread man turned around. The old man, the old woman, the boy, and the girl were still after him and gaining fast.

Fox: Are they after you?

Gingerbread Man: Yes!

Fox: What will you do?

Gingerbread Man: I don't know!

Narrator: The fox pretended to think. He was really planning how to trap the gingerbread man for himself. He draped his furry paw around the gingerbread man's shoulders.

Fox: Maybe I can help.

Gingerbread Man: How?

©1997 Good Apple

Fox: We can swim across the river.

Gingerbread Man: But I can't swim.

Narrator: The fox pretended to think some more. Meanwhile, the gingerbread man saw that his pursuers were getting very close.

Old Man: Let's get him!

Old Woman: Run!

Boy: He can't get away!

Girl: Faster!

Narrator: The fox secretly loved the smell of gingerbread and knew that he had to eat the gingerbread man up all by himself before anyone else could.

Fox: I will help you.

Gingerbread Man: How?

Fox: Climb on my back.

Narrator: And so the gingerbread man did. The fox waded into the river.

Gingerbread Man: The water is wet. I will melt.

©1997 Good Apple

Fox: No, you won't. Climb onto my head.

Narrator: And so the gingerbread man did. The fox began swimming. The gingerbread man looked back. The old man, the old woman, the boy, and the girl were left behind. As the gingerbread man laughed, a wave splashed him.

Gingerbread Man: The water is wet! I will melt!

Fox: No, you won't. Climb onto my nose.

Narrator: And so the gingerbread man did. The fox swam quickly. He was almost across the river when the delicious gingerbread aroma got the better of him.

Fox: Goodbye, gingerbread man.

Gingerbread Man: What?

Narrator: The fox opened his mouth and *snap*! The gingerbread man was gone. Just like that. The fox climbed onto the river bank, patted his stomach, and ran into the forest. The old man, the old woman, the boy, and the girl sadly watched the fox get away with their magnificent gingerbread man. The old woman invited everyone back to the cottage for regular gingerbread cookies, and they all lived happily ever after. Everyone, of course, except for the gingerbread man.

THE THREE LITTLE PIGS

WORD LIST

all	going	money	that
are	goodbye	my	then
bad	hair	never	there
big	hard	not	this
blow	have	of	to
but	he'll	on	too
can	hear	out	us
can't	here	outside	want
care	him	pig	we
chimney	home	pigs	what's
chin	house	puff	where
chinny	huff	run	who's
cold	in	smell	will
dinner	is	some	wolf
do	it	stay	won't
done	it's	sticks	work
down	let	stopped	you
for	let's	straw	your
get	little	sure	
glad	mama	take	
go	me	thank	

THE THREE LITTLE PIGS

CHARACTERS	PROPS
Narrator	bricks
Mama Pig	bundle of straw
Pig 1	bundle of sticks
Pig 2	broom
Pig 3	
Wolf	

Narrator: Once upon a time, a mama pig lived on the edge of the forest with her three little piglets. The day came when the piglets could no longer fit into mama pig's house.

Mama Pig: You are too big for my house!

Pig 1: Not me!

Pig 2: It's *not* me!

Pig 3: I want to stay!

Mama Pig: You are all too big. Here is some money.

Pig 1: Thank you, Mama Pig.

Pig 2: Thank you, Mama.

Pig 3: I want to stay!

Narrator: Mama Pig was not that easily fooled. She pointed to the door.

Mama Pig: All out!

Pig 1: Goodbye, Mama Pig.

Pig 2: Goodbye, Mama.

Pig 3: I want to stay!

Narrator: The three little pigs left their cozy pigsty and went out into the cold, cruel world. They soon discovered that they would need shelter.

Pig 1: I am cold.

Pig 2: Me, too.

Pig 3: I want to go home!

Narrator: Luckily, the three little pigs were walking past a hardware store. They remembered that their mother had given them some money.

Pig 1: I will buy some straw for a house.

Pig 2: I will buy some sticks for a house.

Pig 3: I want to go home!

Narrator: After a lot of arguing, the two bigger pigs convinced the littlest pig to buy some bricks for a house. They stored the sticks and bricks in the shed and got busy building the house of straw.

Pig 1: This is hard work.

Pig 2: It sure is.

Pig 3: I want to go home!

Narrator: Building with straw actually proved to be easier than they thought. They finished the first little pig's house in no time and moved right in.

Pig 1: I am glad that my house is done.

Pig 2: You have a good house.

Pig 3: I want to go home!

Narrator: Somehow, the biggest pig convinced the littlest pig to stick it out. They were relaxing one evening, after putting the last bit of straw on the roof, when they heard a commotion in the yard.

Pig 1: What was that?

Pig 2: Who's there?

Pig 3: I want to go home!

Narrator: It was the big bad wolf!

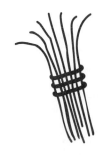  

Wolf: It is the big bad wolf! Let me in, little pigs!

Narrator: Of course, the pigs were scared. Who wouldn't be? Wolves are known to have very big teeth and very large appetites. This is the first lesson little pigs are taught by their mothers.

Pig 1: We won't let you in.

Pig 2: Never.

Pig 3: Not by the hair on my chinny chin chin. I want to go home!

Narrator: Their bad manners made the wolf very mad.

Wolf: Then I'll huff and I'll puff and I'll blow your house down!

Narrator: And he huffed and he puffed and he blew the house down.

Pig 1: Let's get out of here!

Pig 2: Run!

Pig 3: I want to go home!

Narrator: Actually, the three little pigs did go home for a while, but they were bigger than ever, and there simply was no room for all four pigs in Mama Pig's sty.

©1997 Good Apple

Mama Pig: You have to go.

Pig 1: But there's a wolf outside!

Pig 2: He'll get us!

Pig 3: I want to stay!

Narrator: Mama Pig kicked them out anyway. They had no choice but to begin building again. Fortunately, they still had the sticks in the shed, and they started on a second house.

Pig 1: This is hard work.

Pig 2: It sure is.

Pig 3: I want to go home!

Narrator: Since they had practiced with straw, the stick house was a bit easier to build. They settled in. Suddenly they heard a dreadful noise in the yard.

Pig 1: What's that?

Pig 2: Who's there?

Pig 3: I want to go home!

Narrator: It was the big bad wolf. He was *not* in a good mood. He had gotten rather hungry.

Wolf: It is the big bad wolf. Let me in, little pigs!

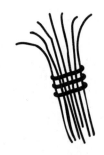  

Narrator: Naturally, letting the wolf in was unreasonable. And the three little pigs told him so.

Pig 1: We won't let you in.

Pig 2: Never.

Pig 3: Not by the hair on my chinny chin chin. I want to go home!

Narrator: The wolf was furious!

Wolf: Then I'll huff and I'll puff and I'll blow your house down.

Narrator: And he did.

Pig 1: Let's get out of here!

Pig 2: Run!

Pig 3: I want to go home!

Narrator: Mama Pig wasn't really pleased to have them crowd back into her little pigsty. The three little pigs didn't even offer to pay rent, and they ate all the slops before anyone could have thirds. Finally she could stand no more.

Mama Pig: You have to go.

Pig 1: But there's a wolf out there!

Pig 2: He will get us!

Pig 3: I want to stay!

Narrator: But Mama Pig pushed them out the pigsty gate. Remembering the bricks in the shed, the three little pigs got busy on a third house.

Pig 1: This is hard work.

Pig 2: It sure is.

Pig 3: I want to go home.

Narrator: Soon the brick house was done, and it looked great. No sooner had they moved in than they heard a terrifying noise in the yard.

Pig 1: What's that?

Pig 2: Who's there?

Pig 3: I want to go home!

Narrator: It was the wolf! His mood was awful. He hadn't had a good porkchop, slice of ham, rasher of bacon, or even a ham hock in quite some time and he was ravenous.

Wolf: It is the big bad wolf. Let me in, little pigs!

Narrator: How could they?

©1997 Good Apple

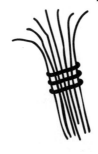  

Pig 1: We won't let you in.

Pig 2: Never.

Pig 3: Not by the hair on my chinny chin chin.
I want to go home!

Narrator: The wolf wasn't about to let such rudeness pass, especially when he was so very hungry.

Wolf: Then I'll huff and I'll puff and I'll blow your house down.

Narrator: Well, he huffed and he puffed and he huffed and he puffed until his asthma finally kicked in and he had to rest.

Pig 1: He stopped!

Pig 2: Let's run!

Pig 3: I want to go home!

Narrator: The pigs decided, much against the littlest pig's wishes, to stay and outwit the wolf. So they filled a big black cauldron with water and placed it over the fire in the chimney. It began to boil. The wolf sat up and sniffed the air.

Wolf: I smell dinner.

Narrator: And the wolf climbed onto the roof of the little pigs' house.

Pig 1: I hear the wolf!

Pig 2: Me, too.

Pig 3: I want to go home!

Narrator: The wolf dove into the chimney headfirst. After skipping so many meals, he was just skinny enough to slide down the chimney flue. Unfortunately for the pigs, they had forgotten to uncover the cauldron, and the wolf hit the iron cover—*kerwham*—and knocked himself out. Fortunately, the little pigs were smart enough to run away before the wolf came to.

Pig 1: Where can we go?

Pig 2: What will we do?

Pig 3: Let's go home.

Narrator: And so they did. You can imagine their mother's reaction.

Mama Pig: What's going on?

Pig 1: The wolf is in the chimney.

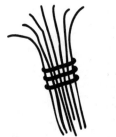  

Pig 2: He's out cold.

Pig 3: Can't we stay?

Narrator: Mama Pig was so fed up with the three little pigs that she grabbed a broom and marched out of the sty.

Mama Pig: I'll take care of him.

Narrator: And she did. When she got to the little pigs' house, she was feeling much madder and stronger than the dizzy, starved wolf. She whacked him right out of the house and into the forest.

Mama Pig: There.

Narrator: The wolf recovered from the beating and lived long enough to make trouble in another tale. The three little pigs were able to move back into the brick house, where they lived happily ever after.

©1997 Good Apple

CHICKEN LICKEN

WORD LIST

a	help	oh
am	Henny	on
are	here	out
be	hit	Penny
calling	how	piece
chicken	hungry	right
close	I	safe
come	in	sky
dear	is	someone
dears	it	sure
do	know	that
Ducky	let's	the
eat	Licken	to
falling	listen	Turkey
farmer's	Loosey	us
follow	Loxy	wanted
fox	Lucky	was
Foxy	Lurkey	we
get	matter	what
Goosey	me	wife
have	must	will
head	my	yes
hear	of	you

CHICKEN LICKEN

CHARACTERS	PROPS
Narrator	apron
Chicken Licken	acorn
Henny Penny	box for a cave
Ducky Lucky	
Goosey Loosey	
Turkey Lurkey	
Foxy Loxy	

Narrator: Once upon a time on a farm in a faraway land, a careless farmhand left the gate open, and all the farm birds got loose. One of them, Chicken Licken, was minding her own business, scratching around for seeds on the forest floor, when an acorn fell from an oak tree and conked her on the head. The fact that an acorn fell wasn't so unusual because it was autumn, but it *was* unusual to hit someone so squarely on the head. Now, Chicken Licken was a daffy sort of bird, and she came to all the wrong conclusions.

Chicken Licken: The sky is falling! Help!

Narrator: Being a featherbrained bird, Chicken Licken ran screaming through the woods instead of looking around for what had hit her.

©1997 Good Apple

Chicken Licken: Help! Help!

Narrator: Her cries alarmed her friend Henny Penny.

Henny Penny: What is the matter?

Chicken Licken: The sky is falling!

Henny Penny: How do you know?

Chicken Licken: A piece of it hit me on my head.

Henny Penny: What! We must get help.

Narrator: Together, they ran on, clucking for help. Their screams awakened their friend Ducky Lucky.

Henny Penny: Help! Help!

Ducky Lucky: What is the matter?

Chicken Licken: The sky is falling!

Ducky Lucky: How do you know?

Chicken Licken: A piece of it hit me on my head.

Henny Penny: We must get help!

Narrator: So the three foolish fowls scurried off, feathers flying, in search of help.

Ducky Lucky: Help! Help!

Henny Penny: Someone help us!

Narrator: Of course, their cries were heard by their companion Goosey Loosey.

Ducky Lucky: Help!

Henny Penny: You have to help!

Chicken Licken: The sky is falling!

Goosey Loosey: What?

Chicken Licken: The sky is falling!

Goosey Loosey: How do you know?

Chicken Licken: A piece of it hit me on my head.

Goosey Loosey: We must get help!

Narrator: So the four hysterical friends flapped their wings and squawked, dashing to and fro, not knowing which way to turn.

Goosey Loosey: Help!

Ducky Lucky: Oh, dear!

Henny Penny: Someone help!

Chicken Licken: The sky is falling!

Narrator: All the clucking disturbed their pal Turkey Lurkey, who was busy pecking at some seeds.

Turkey Lurkey: What is the matter?

Chicken Licken: The sky is falling!

Turkey Lurkey: How do you know?

Chicken Licken: A piece of it hit me on my head.

Turkey Lurkey: We must get help!

Narrator: Now, five disturbed fowls make a great deal of noise, and the noise brought the attention of a hungry forest animal.

Foxy Loxy: I am Foxy Loxy.

Narrator: Foxy Loxy hadn't had a good chicken dinner in quite a while, so he was very interested in what the commotion was about.

Foxy Loxy: I am hungry.

Narrator: Being a clever sort of fellow, Foxy Loxy disguised himself as an old woman and went in search of his dinner. The frenzied fowls were very easily found.

Chicken Licken: The sky is falling!

Henny Penny: Help!

Ducky Lucky: Oh, dear!

Goosey Loosey: Someone help!

Turkey Lurkey: Oh, my!

Narrator: Foxy Loxy cleared his throat to get their attention and made his voice sound old-womanish.

Foxy Loxy: What is the matter, my dears?

Chicken Licken: The sky is falling!

Foxy Loxy: How do you know?

Chicken Licken: A piece of it hit me on my head.

Foxy Loxy: What?

Narrator: Foxy Loxy looked up. All he saw was the beautiful blue sky. His stomach growled, and his mind cleared. Dinner was near.

Foxy Loxy: I am sure you are right. We must get help. Follow me.

Narrator: Of course, the birds followed Foxy Loxy, since his disguise made him look exactly like a harmless old woman. They followed him right to his den.

Foxy Loxy: Come in, Turkey Lurkey.

Turkey Lurkey: Will I be safe?

Foxy Loxy: Yes.

Narrator: Turkey Lurkey went into the fox's lair and didn't come out.

Foxy Loxy: Come in, Goosey Loosey.

Goosey Loosey: Will I be safe?

Foxy Loxy: Yes.

Narrator: And Goosey Loosey went in. She didn't come out, either.

Foxy Loxy: Come in, Ducky Lucky.

Ducky Lucky: Will I be safe?

Foxy Loxy: Yes.

Narrator: Guess what happened? Ducky Lucky went in and didn't come out.

Foxy Loxy: Come in, Henny Penny.

Henny Penny: Will I be safe?

Foxy Loxy: Yes.

Narrator: She too went into the fox's cave and didn't come out.

Foxy Loxy: Come in, Chicken Licken.

Chicken Licken: Will I be safe?

Foxy Loxy: Yes.

Narrator: Just then, the wind blew extra hard, and a large acorn hit the fox squarely on the top of his head. What a coincidence! He stared up at the sky, exposing his long, sharp teeth to Chicken Licken.

Foxy Loxy: What was that?

©1997 Good Apple

Narrator: Chicken Licken wised up. *Now* she knew what had knocked her on the head. And she knew that she was in terrible danger, for she had seen the fox's teeth and had glimpsed the fox's fur beneath his clever disguise.

Chicken Licken: It was a piece of the sky.

Foxy Loxy: It was?

Chicken Licken: Yes. You must run for help!

Narrator: And so the fox ran off seeking assistance. As soon as he was out of sight, Chicken Licken flew into the fox's cave and saved her feathered friends.

Henny Penny: It was the fox!

Ducky Lucky: Help!

Goosey Loosey: He wanted to eat us!

Turkey Lurkey: Listen! I hear the farmer's wife calling us!

Chicken Licken: Let's get out of here!

Narrator: The friends scurried home as fast as they could and were grateful when the farmer's wife locked the gate behind them.

Chicken Licken: That was close!

Narrator: As far as I know, Foxy Loxy is still looking for help. The farmyard birds never dared go into the forest again, and they all lived happily ever after.

THE THREE BILLY GOATS GRUFF

WORD LIST

a	don't	I	that
across	eat	is	the
afraid	fatter	it	there
am	feet	let	think
and	fierce	little	this
are	first	look	tiptoe
at	for	maybe	to
be	forget	me	too
before	gee	medium	troll
big	get	my	up
bigger	go	not	very
billy	goat	now	wait
bridge	going	oh	want
brother	Gruff	on	we
but	have	only	who
by	he	pass	why
can	hear	please	will
can't	heard	ready	wow
come	help	right	yes
comes	here	run	you
did	hill	safe	your
dinner	him	see	
do	hungry	than	

©1997 Good Apple

THE THREE BILLY GOATS GRUFF

CHARACTERS

Narrator
Big Goat
Medium Goat
Little Goat
Troll

PROPS

cardboard bridge
blue craft paper water
grass
paper snow

Narrator: Once upon a time, three goats, all named Gruff, lived happily in a beautiful mountain meadow. There was a big billy goat, a medium-sized goat, and a little goat.

Big Goat: I am the big goat.

Medium Goat: I am the medium goat.

Little Goat: And I am the little goat.

Narrator: When winter came and the snow fell, all their grass was covered up, and they grew very hungry.

Big Goat: I am hungry.

Medium Goat: I am, too.

Little Goat: Don't forget me!

Narrator: They all decided to go down the mountain for grass. There were only two little problems with their plan. One—they weren't crazy about crossing bridges, and two—the bridge they had to cross to get down the mountain belonged to a fierce troll.

Troll: I am the fierce troll!

Narrator: But the goats were very hungry and decided to try their luck in spite of the bridge problem.

Big Goat: I am very hungry.

Medium Goat: I am, too.

Little Goat: Don't forget me!

Narrator: The goats argued for a while and then decided to send the little billy goat down the mountain first, even though he was terrified.

Big Goat: The troll will not hear your little feet on the bridge.

Medium Goat: You will get by.

Little Goat: I don't want to be first!

Narrator: The big goat and the medium goat shoved the little billy goat Gruff on down the mountain, anyway.

Little Goat: Maybe I can tiptoe across.

©1997 Good Apple

Narrator: So he tried crossing the bridge on tiptoe. His little feet went *trip, trap, trip, trap, trip, trap*—very quietly. Unfortunately the troll was not only fierce, but he also had sharp ears.

Troll: Who is on my bridge?

Narrator: The little billy goat Gruff was paralyzed with fear.

Little Goat: It is only little billy goat Gruff.

Narrator: The troll licked his lips.

Troll: I will eat you up.

Narrator: The little billy goat Gruff shook so hard that his feet rattled on the wooden bridge like sleet on windowpanes.

Little Goat: Please don't eat me!

Troll: Why not?

Narrator: The little billy goat Gruff had to do some really quick thinking. Remembering how his brothers had rudely pushed him down the hill first, he came up with a plan to get back at them.

Little Goat: I have a big brother.

Troll: You do?

Little Goat: He is bigger than I am.

Troll: He is?

Little Goat: Yes, and fatter, too.

Troll: Oh?

Little Goat: Why don't you wait for him?

Troll: I think I will.

Narrator: So the troll crept back under the bridge. The little billy goat Gruff wiped the sweat from his forehead and ran across the bridge as fast as he could.

Little Goat: I am safe now!

Narrator: The two bigger goats saw that their little brother had crossed the bridge without getting eaten by the troll.

Big Goat: Did you see that?

Medium Goat: Yes. The troll let him pass.

Big Goat: Why can't we?

Medium Goat: Why not?

Narrator: Then they had a big quarrel about who would try to cross the bridge next.

Big Goat: You are going!

Medium Goat: Not me.

Big Goat: Oh, yes, you are!

Narrator: Naturally, the biggest goat was also the strongest goat. The medium goat Gruff got pushed down the hill, kicking and screaming, while the big billy goat Gruff snickered behind his hoof.

Medium Goat: I don't want to go!

Big Goat: But you will.

Narrator: The medium billy goat Gruff slid to a stop just before his hooves touched the wooden bridge. He looked around carefully for the troll. He looked hard, but the troll was well hidden.

Medium Goat: Maybe I can tiptoe across.

Narrator: He began crossing the bridge on tiptoe. His feet went *trip, trap, trip, trap, trip, trap*. Of course, the troll heard and jumped right out.

Troll: Who is on my bridge?

Narrator: The medium billy goat Gruff began to tremble with fear. His teeth clacked together.

Medium Goat: It is only medium billy goat Gruff.

Narrator: The troll rubbed his tummy.

Troll: I will eat you.

Narrator: Medium billy goat Gruff's teeth chattered even louder and his eyes rolled back in his head. He thought he might actually faint.

Medium Goat: Please don't eat me!

Troll: Why not?

Narrator: Medium billy goat Gruff recalled how his big brother had snickered behind his hoof, while he, medium billy goat Gruff, had brushed snow out of his coat where he had fallen. Medium billy goat Gruff thought fast and came up with a plan.

Medium Goat: I have a big brother.

Troll: I have heard this before.

Medium Goat: I do! He is bigger than I am.

Troll: He is?

Medium Goat: Yes, and fatter, too.

Troll: Oh?

Medium Goat: Can you see him up there on the hill?

Narrator: Now the troll had great ears and an undiscriminating appetite, but lousy vision. He really needed glasses but was too vain to get them. He squinted, but he couldn't see the big white goat against the white snow.

Troll: I can't see him.

Medium Goat: He's right there.

Narrator: Medium billy goat Gruff pointed up the mountainside.

Medium Goat: Why don't you wait for him?

Troll: Maybe I will.

Narrator: The troll thought about ambushing the medium billy goat and eating him anyway, but being a greedy fellow, he decided to take a chance that, indeed, a more sumptuous meal was about to come his way. He hid under the bridge while the medium billy goat Gruff scurried across the bridge with a huge sigh of relief.

Medium Goat: Safe!

Narrator: Now the big billy goat Gruff spied both his brothers down in the green grass while he was still knee-deep in snow and getting hungrier by the second. He snorted and pawed the snow.

Big Goat: I am not afraid.

Narrator: To tell the truth, he probably was—just a bit.

Big Goat: I am bigger than the troll.

Narrator: He pawed more snow. It flew into the sky in an arc behind him.

Big Goat: I am very hungry!

Narrator: So, the big goat kicked up his hooves and charged down the hill, his dangerous horns lowered.

Big Goat: Here I come!

Narrator: The little billy goat and the medium billy goat felt the earth tremble under their hooves, and they crowded together on the far side of the bridge. They sensed a great battle coming and didn't want to miss one minute of the entertainment.

Little Goat: Here comes big billy goat!

Medium Goat: Look at him run!

Narrator: The troll, of course, having very good ears, heard the billy goat coming and sprang up on the bridge to block the way.

Troll: I am ready for dinner!

Big Goat: Me, too!

Narrator: The big billy goat's hooves thundered over the bridge. The troll flexed his muscles and snarled. Indeed, a magnificent battle took place. The goat's hair flew as the troll kicked and bit. But the big billy goat Gruff had had practice fighting with his brothers, and the troll had been an only child. Troll hair flew as the billy goat butted, kicked, and bit.

Little Goat: Wow!

Medium Goat: Gee!

Narrator: Well, after an hour or so, the big billy goat's horns snagged the troll's pants, and big billy goat Gruff tossed him high into the air and off the bridge. The troll landed *kersplat* in the cold, swift river.

Big Goat: I can eat now. And I am *hungry*!

Narrator: And he too went over the bridge into the green pasture.

Troll: Help!

Narrator: The troll did not get his goat meal that day. As a matter of fact, it took him a few days to swim back to his home under the bridge. But the three billy goats Gruff lived happily ever after—until they had to cross the bridge again.

HANSEL AND GRETEL

WORD LIST

a	flashlight	make	there
am	for	map	this
and	free	me	time
are	gee	melting	to
back	get	mother	today
be	give	must	trick
been	go	my	true
berries	Gretel	new	unhappy
boohoo	Hansel	nibbling	up
boy	have	no	us
brought	help	not	wanted
but	her	now	was
cage	here	nuts	way
can't	him	okay	we
children	home	on	what
come	honey	papa	where
compass	house	rid	who
cook	I	right	why
could	I'm	she	will
dark	in	some	witch
do	into	something	witch's
eat	is	stay	with
enough	it	stew	work
fat	let's	thank	wow
fatten	look	that	yes
feed	lost	the	you
find	lucky	them	yum

Hansel and Gretel

CHARACTERS	PROPS
Narrator	compass
Hansel	map
Gretel	flashlight
Papa	box for a cage
Stepmother	ax
Witch	bone

Narrator: Once upon a time, a little boy named Hansel, a little girl named Gretel, and their loving papa lived in a small cottage near a great wood.

Hansel: I am Hansel.

Gretel: I am Gretel.

Papa: And I am the papa.

Narrator: One day, quite unexpectedly, Papa brought home a new wife. Hansel and Gretel didn't even know that he'd been dating!

Stepmother: I am the new mother.

Narrator: Unfortunately the new stepmother and the children didn't get along very well, and everyone was quite miserable.

Hansel: I am unhappy.

Gretel: I am unhappy.

Papa: I am unhappy.

Stepmother: I must do something.

Narrator: No one knows why she did it, but one day, the stepmother told the children a big fat lie—perhaps hoping to bring peace to the household.

Stepmother: You will get some nuts.

Hansel: Okay with me.

Gretel: Okay, we will.

Narrator: And she led them deep into the woods and left them there. Being good children, Hansel and Gretel gathered as many nuts as they could carry.

Hansel: This is enough.

Gretel: Yes.

Narrator: Then they realized that they were all alone. Gretel began to cry.

Gretel: Boohoo! We are lost.

Hansel: Lucky for us, I brought a compass.

Narrator: Indeed he had. His Boy Scout training had come in handy. And using the compass skillfully, the children made it back home safely.

Stepmother: You are back!

Hansel: Yes.

Gretel: Here are the nuts.

Papa: Thank you, my children.

Narrator: The stepmother left the children alone for several days. And then the arguments began again. She decided to tell another big fat lie.

Stepmother: You will get some berries.

Hansel: Okay with me.

Gretel: Okay, we will.

Narrator: She led them deeper into the woods again and crept off while they were busy gathering berries.

Hansel: This is enough.

Gretel: Yes.

©1997 Good Apple

Narrator: And then they knew that they were all alone again. The sky was already darkening, and spooky sounds came from all around them. Gretel began to cry.

Gretel: Boohoo! We are lost.

Hansel: Lucky for us, I brought a map and a flashlight.

Narrator: Indeed he had. Again, he used his head and his Boy Scout training, and they made it safely back home. It was very late when they arrived.

Stepmother: You are back.

Hansel: Yes.

Gretel: Here are the berries.

Papa: Thank you, my children.

Narrator: The stepmother tossed and turned all night, dreading the next quarrel the little family was sure to have. And then she had a wicked idea.

Stepmother: I will give them to the witch!

Narrator: It was a mean plan, but do it she did. The very next day, the stepmother told a whopping big lie to the children.

Stepmother: You will get some honey.

Hansel: Okay with me.

Gretel: Okay, we will.

Narrator: The stepmother led Hansel and Gretel farther into the forest than they'd ever been before. When they stopped for a drink of water, she vanished, and the children were alone. Now, being good children, they looked for the honey, but there was none. It began to get dark, and Gretel became frightened.

Gretel: Boohoo! We are lost.

Narrator: This time, Hansel had to agree. He searched his pockets for the compass and the map and the flashlight, but they weren't there.

Hansel: Yes. This time we *are* lost.

Narrator: Just as they were about to despair, Hansel climbed a tree, hoping to figure out where they were. He noticed a light shining among the trees a short distance away.

Hansel: Look!

Narrator: Hansel and Gretel set off through the woods. Soon they discovered the source of the light.

Hansel: It is a house.

Gretel: And what a house!

Narrator: The house sparkled as the light reflected off gumdrop windowpanes, icing shingles, and jellybean shutters. The walls gave off the aroma of freshly-baked gingerbread, and the smoke scented the air with cinnamon. For the house they saw was built of cookies and candy!

Hansel: Wow!

Gretel: Gee!

Narrator: After wandering in the woods all day, naturally Hansel and Gretel were hungry. They couldn't resist a nibble here and a bite there from the delicious house.

Hansel: Yum.

Gretel: Yum, yum.

Narrator: Suddenly the door burst open, and a witch appeared!

Witch: Who is nibbling on my house?

Hansel: It is Hansel and Gretel.

Gretel: Boohoo!

©1997 Good Apple

Narrator: The witch saw an opportunity for child stew—her favorite dish—and one she hadn't had the chance to have lately. So she allowed the children to fill up on bits and pieces of her house. When they could eat no more, and needed a good dose of pink medicine for their stomachaches, she smiled a witchy smile.

Witch: Come in, children.

Hansel: We can't.

Witch: Why not?

Gretel: We have to go home.

Witch: But it is dark.

Hansel: That is true.

Witch: You will get lost.

Gretel: Hansel, she is right.

Narrator: And that was how the witch coaxed them into her house. Once they were in, she slammed the door, pushed Gretel into a corner, and locked Hansel in a cage. She pointed to Gretel.

Witch: There. You will do work.

Narrator: She pointed to Hansel.

Witch: And you will get fat for my stew.

Narrator: Hansel and Gretel knew they were in really big trouble. Try as he might, Hansel couldn't get Gretel to leave the witch's house and get help. Even though she had always been a bit of a crybaby, she was determined to stay by her brother.

Hansel: Go home.

Gretel: I will not.

Hansel: She will eat you.

Gretel: No, we will trick her.

Narrator: Where Gretel found courage when before she had found only tears, we will never know. But she proved to be just as clever as Hansel.

Witch: We will fatten him up.

Gretel: Okay. I will feed him.

Narrator: Now the witch had very poor eyesight, and for some strange reason, she trusted Gretel. So when the witch gave Gretel food for Hansel, Gretel tossed most of it out the window. And when the witch reached in the cage to pinch Hansel to check if he was fat enough for her stew, he always let her feel an old bone. The witch was fooled into believing that he needed more fattening. The trick gave them just enough time to make a plan.

Hansel: We can not stay here.

Gretel: No.

Hansel: You have to get rid of her.

Gretel: What?

Hansel: You will find a way.

Narrator: The next day, the witch told Gretel she planned to put Hansel into the stew pot for supper whether he was fat enough or not. Gretel went straight to Hansel with the information while the witch was outside gathering vegetables from her garden.

Gretel: She will cook you today.

©1997 Good Apple

Hansel and Gretel ■ 81

Hansel: You must do something.

Gretel: But what?

Narrator: Hansel had no answers. The witch pulled out her huge stew pot and built a great fire under it. She filled it with water and put in onions, carrots, and potatoes. She licked her greedy, witchy lips.

Witch: Now for Hansel!

Hansel: Do something!

Gretel: What?

Witch: Boy stew! Yum!

Hansel: Help!

Narrator: What else could Gretel do? She gave the witch a swift karate chop and pushed her into the stew pot. Gretel slammed down the lid.

Witch: Help! I'm melting!

Narrator: It didn't take long for the witch to melt into nothingness. Of course, the children didn't care to stay for supper. Gretel unlocked Hansel's prison, and they ran out of the beautiful gingerbread house.

Gretel: You are free!

Hansel: Yes!

Narrator: Far off in the woods, they heard the sound of an ax.

Hansel: It could be Papa!

Gretel: Let's go!

Narrator: Sure enough, it was their loving Papa out chopping wood for the fire. He was as overjoyed to see them as they were to see him.

Papa: Hansel! Gretel! Where have you been?

Hansel: In the witch's house!

Gretel: Hansel was in a cage!

Hansel: She wanted to make me into stew!

Narrator: On and on they chattered until their story was told. Papa broke the witch's house into cookies with his ax, and they ate it all up. It took them two years to do it. As for the lying stepmother, well, she left the minute the children returned and was never seen again. And Hansel and Gretel and their papa lived happily ever after.

©1997 Good Apple

THE BREMEN TOWN MUSICIANS

WORD LIST

a	giant	maybe	the
am	go	me	there
an	going	meow	they
are	good	mice	think
at	have	milk	this
bones	he	more	tired
bowwow	heehaw	morning	to
branches	help	my	too
but	here	near	top
cannot	him	need	tree
chase	hiss	night	tree's
city	hits	not	under
clawed	hunt	of	us
cock-a-	I	old	very
doodle-doo	in	out	voice
cold	is	plan	wake
come	it	roof	we
cook	just	room	what
do	kicked	said	where
donkey	kitchen	scraps	will
down	leg	see	witch
face	let's	she	with
family	light	shed	woof
far	little	sing	wow
feast	living	sleep	yard
fire	log	some	you
food	look	sounds	yum
for	man	spot	
get	matches	stabbed	
getting	matter	stew	

THE BREMEN TOWN MUSICIANS

CHARACTERS	PROPS
Narrator	table
Donkey	food
Dog	shoe box
Cat	costume jewelry
Rooster	play money
Thief	water

Narrator: Once upon a time, there was a donkey who had become too old to work in the fields. One day, he overheard his master talking about getting rid of him forever.

Donkey: I am an old donkey, but I have a good voice. I will go to the city to sing.

Narrator: So the old donkey trotted down the road. Before long, he came upon an old dog lying in the road.

Donkey: What is the matter?

Dog: I am old. I cannot hunt. What will I do?

Donkey: You can come with me. I am going to the city to sing.

Dog: I think I will.

Narrator: So off they walked together. Pretty soon they saw an old cat sitting in the middle of the road.

Donkey: What is the matter?

Cat: I am old.
I cannot chase mice.
What will I do?

Donkey: You can come with us.
We are going to the city to sing.

Cat: I think I will.

Narrator: On they went—the cat, the dog, and the donkey. Soon they passed a farm. An old rooster flew into the road and fluffed his feathers sadly.

Donkey: What is the matter?

Rooster: I am old.
I cannot wake the family.
What will I do?

Donkey: You can come with us.
We are going to the city to sing.

Rooster: I think I will.

Narrator: As they went down the road, the four friends discussed what fine musicians they would become. When night fell, they left the road to find food and shelter for the evening.

Donkey: I will sleep near this tree.

Dog: I will sleep in this log.

Cat: I will sleep in the tree's branches.

Rooster: I will sleep at the top of the tree.

Narrator: When the rooster got to the top of the tree, he looked all around for signs of danger. He saw nothing dangerous, but he did see a light way off in the woods.

Rooster: I see a light.

Dog: What is it?

Cat: Is it far?

Donkey: Let's go!
It is very cold here.

Narrator: So off they went in the direction of the light.

Donkey: Maybe there is a shed for me.

Dog: Maybe there are some bones for me.

Cat: Maybe there is some milk for me.

Rooster: Maybe there are some scraps for me.

Narrator: As they neared the light, the friends saw a house. The donkey, being the tallest, looked in the window.

Dog: What do you see?

Rooster: Is there food?

Cat: Is there a fire?

Narrator: What the donkey saw was a thief's hideaway. The house held stolen jewels and chests of money, as well as food and water. And the donkey told them so.

Rooster: It sounds good.

Dog: Let's go in.

Donkey: We need a plan.

Narrator: So they put their heads together and came up with a scheme. The donkey stood on his hind legs with his front hooves on the windowsill, the dog got on the donkey's back, the cat climbed onto the dog, and the rooster perched on the cat's back. Then they began to sing.

Donkey: Heehaw! Heehaw!

Dog: Bowwow! Bowwow!

Cat: Meow! Meow!

Rooster: Cock-a-doodle-doo!

Narrator: Then they all jumped through the window at once. They made such a horrible noise that the thief was frightened out of his wits. He ran screaming from the house.

Thief: Help! They will get me!

Narrator: The four friends now had a warm shelter and plenty of good food and water. They ate like pigs.

Donkey: Yum!

Dog: This is good.

Cat: This hits the spot.

Rooster: Is there more?

Narrator: When they were full, the animals settled down for the night. The donkey chose to sleep on the hay in the yard. The dog lay on a mat just inside the door. The cat curled up near the fire. And the rooster sat upon the mantel above the fireplace.

Donkey: What a feast!

Dog: I am tired.

©1997 Good Apple

Cat: Me, too. Go to sleep.

Rooster: I will wake you in the morning. Good night.

Narrator: The animals slept peacefully, but not so the thief. He did not like being scared right out of his house, so he crept back after he'd gotten some courage back. Since the lights were out, he thought the house was empty.

Thief: I will just look inside.

Narrator: So he tiptoed in through the back door.

Thief: Where are my matches?

Narrator: Unfortunately the sound of the thief's voice woke the cat. She stared at him with glittering eyes. Thinking the shiny eyes were embers in the fireplace with which to light his match, the thief reached down into the cat's face, scaring her.

Cat: Hiss!

Narrator: The cat scratched at the thief's face.

Thief: Help!

Narrator: The thief ran for the door. Too bad for him. The dog woke and bit his leg.

Dog: Woof! Grr!

Thief: Help!

Narrator: The thief staggered out into the yard, where his cries woke the donkey. The donkey gave the thief a swift kick that knocked him flat.

Donkey: Heehaw!

Thief: Help!

Narrator: The rooster was very upset by all the noise.

Rooster: Cock-a-doodle-doo!

Narrator: The thief was terrified!

Thief: I am getting out of here!
There is a witch in the kitchen. She clawed at my face!
There is a man in the living room. He stabbed my leg!
There is a giant in the yard. He kicked me down!
And there is a little man on the roof. He said, "Cook him in a stew!"

Narrator: So the thief went away and never came back. The four musical friends enjoyed their new house so much that they never traveled on to the city. They stayed where they were and lived happily ever after.

LITTLE RED RIDING HOOD

WORD LIST

a	good	no	the
am	Grandma	not	then
are	Grandma's	now	there
bad	have	of	this
besides	hear	oh	to
better	hello	on	too
big	here	ouch	up
book	house	out	very
can	how	quiet	was
chicken	I	red	we
close	I'll	Red's	what
cold	I'm	right	will
come	in	see	with
could	is	send	wolf
course	it	smell	won't
door	let's	some	would
ears	like	something	yes
eat	little	sorry	you
eyes	love	soup	your
feeling	missed	supper	
fool	mother	take	
go	my	teeth	
going	new	that	

LITTLE RED RIDING HOOD

CHARACTERS	PROPS
Narrator	ice pack
Mother	book
Little Red	basket
Grandma	soup can
Wolf	flower
	red cape
	shawl
	phone

Narrator: Once upon a time, a little girl and her mother lived near a very dark wood. The girl's nickname was Little Red Riding Hood, probably because her mother's favorite color was red, and that was all she ever chose for her daughter when she went shopping. All that red no doubt made Little Red's temper a bit short and unpredictable.

Mother: I am Little Red's mother. I love red.

Little Red: I am Little Red. I would like something besides red.

Narrator: Let's put all that aside for now, though. One day, Little Red's mother got a phone call.

Mother: Hello?

Grandma: This is Grandma.

Mother: Yes.

Grandma: I have a cold.

Mother: I'm sorry.

Grandma: Could you send Little Red with some chicken soup?

Mother: Of course.

Narrator: And so, Mother dragged Little Red away from a book she was reading and placed a basket of crackers and hot chicken soup in her arms.

Mother: Take this to Grandma.

Little Red: Now?

Mother: Yes.

Narrator: So Little Red marked her place in the book and reluctantly put on her red cape. Now Grandma lived deep in the dark wood at the end of a path. Little Red would have rather been reading, of course, but she took off anyway with the basket and a bad attitude. She knew Grandma would probably be on the phone, so she tucked her book in the basket, too.

Little Red: Here I go.

Narrator: As everyone knows, woods are the habitat for wolves. And in this particular wood, there lived an evil and very hungry wolf. As Little Red passed his lair, he got a good whiff of chicken soup.

©1997 Good Apple

Wolf: I smell soup!

Narrator: He licked his lips and began to follow Little Red, keeping carefully in the brush. Little Red sang to herself as she walked.

Little Red: I am going to Grandma's house.

Wolf: Grandma's house?

Narrator: Suddenly the wolf had a brilliant idea. He would beat Little Red to Grandma's house, for he knew the way and four legs are faster than two.

Wolf: I will eat Grandma.
I will eat Little Red.
And I will eat the soup.

Narrator: The little girl skipped on down the path, and the wolf raced for Grandma's house. When he arrived and peeked in the window, he saw Grandma in bed with an ice pack on her head.

Wolf: Supper!

Narrator: He jumped in the window and snarled at Grandma.

Wolf: I will eat you!

Grandma: Oh, no, you won't!

Narrator: And Grandma belted him a good one on his tender nose with her ice pack. She just barely made it to the closet and slammed the door in the wolf's face before his jaws snapped shut.

Wolf: Missed!

Grandma: That was close!

Narrator: And then, the wolf got another brilliant idea. He put on a gown of grandma's and her nightcap, which had fallen off in the scuffle. He climbed into bed and pulled the covers up to his chin.

Wolf: I will fool Little Red.

Grandma: You won't.

Wolf: I will. And then I'll eat you, too!

Narrator: A few minutes later, Little Red walked into Grandma's house.

Little Red: Hello, Grandma.

Wolf: Hello, Little Red.

Little Red: How are you feeling?

Wolf: Bad.

Narrator: Little Red sat near Grandma's bed and handed her the basket.

Little Red: Here is some soup.

Wolf: Good.

Narrator: Little Red looked carefully at her grandmother. Grandma seemed a bit different. Maybe she'd been on the phone too long and was simply exhausted.

Little Red: Grandma, what big eyes you have.

Wolf: The better to see you with.

Little Red: Grandma, what big ears you have.

Wolf: The better to hear you with.

Narrator: The wolf licked his lips. He could hardly wait to begin his feast.

Little Red: Grandma, what big teeth you have.

Narrator: Grandma had had her ear pressed to the closet door all this time and she knew that Little Red was in terrible danger. She did the only thing she could to save her granddaughter.

Grandma: See my new book?

Narrator: Little Red was a bit confused. She thought the voice she heard had come from the closet and not the figure in the bed. She did the only thing she could— being such a good reader.

Little Red: Let's see your new book.

Wolf: What?

Little Red: Your new book!

©1997 Good Apple

Narrator: Now the wolf knew nothing about books because he'd never been to school and had never learned to read. He didn't even know what a book looked like. But he knew that if he didn't get busy eating her, his chance for a meal would be gone forever. He handed Little Red a nearby flower and licked his lips.

Little Red: Let's see the book.

Wolf: Go on. There it is.

Narrator: Little Red was puzzled. She looked closer at the figure in the bed.

Little Red: You are not Grandma!

Wolf: You are right!

Little Red: You are a wolf!

Wolf: Grr! I will eat you up!

Narrator: Little Red instinctively grabbed the heavy book and threw her red cloak over the wolf's face, stopping him for just a minute.

Grandma: Let me out!

Little Red: Let me in!

Wolf: Let me out!

Narrator: The wolf tossed the red cape away and ran after Little Red. She ducked into the closet just as his jaws were about to snap shut. As a little parting gift, she smacked him a good one on his tender nose.

Little Red: There!

Wolf: Ouch!

Grandma: Close the door!

Narrator: Little Red called for help on grandma's portable phone, which Grandma, in her haste to get away from the wolf, had tucked into the pocket of her robe. The wolf snarled at the closet door. He didn't hear the zookeepers behind him until it was too late. They shot him with a tranquilizing dart and trussed him up in a net.

Grandma: Can we come out now?

Little Red: It is very quiet.

Narrator: Later they found out that the wolf had been sent to a zoo in a far-away city. Little Red and Grandma were both relieved and spent many happy hours sharing the books they had. Fortunately for Little Red's temper and wardrobe, Mother bought other colors for her to wear, thereby improving her disposition. And they all lived happily ever after, except, of course, for the wolf, who was forced to eat zoo food for the rest of his life.

CINDERELLA

WORD LIST

a	fairy	midnight	the
all	find	mop	then
am	food	most	there
are	fun	must	this
back	get	my	time
be	girl	new	tired
beautiful	go	not	to
bring	godmother	now	too
but	going	of	try
by	good	oh	up
can	had	on	want
can't	have	one	was
charming	he	party	well
chores	her	prince	what
Cinderella	home	princess	where
close	how	promise	who
coming	hurry	right	why
could	I	scrub	will
course	is	she	with
dancing	it	slipper	won't
didn't	it's	slow	wonderful
dirty	know	so	work
do	lazy	someone	would
does	like	something	yes
don't	lots	stranger	you
dress	lovely	sweep	your
dust	maybe	thank	
either	me	that	

 CINDERELLA

CHARACTERS	PROPS
Narrator	wand
Cinderella	apron
Mother	two paper crowns
Stepsister 1	gown
Stepsister 2	bucket
Fairy Godmother	shoe
Prince	

Narrator: Once upon a time in a land faraway, there lived a girl named Cinderella. She had a regular name, of course, but everyone, even her own mother, had forgotten it.

Cinderella: I am Cinderella.

Narrator: Many months ago, Cinderella and her mother had lived happily in a little cottage in the woods. But when the stepsisters came along, they all moved to a house not far from a lovely palace. And the mother changed into a real shrew.

Mother: Work, girl.

Cinderella: But I am tired.

Mother: So what?

Stepsister 1: Bring my food.

Stepsister 2: Bring my dress.

Stepsister 1: Hurry up, Cinderella.

Stepsister 2: You are so slow.

Narrator: Needless to say, Cinderella was miserable. When the sisters were out having a wonderful time, she was left at home to do all the chores.

Mother: Scrub! Mop! Dust! Sweep!

Cinderella: I will.

Narrator: What else could Cinderella do? She worked very hard every day. One day, a messenger brought news that the prince, who lived in the lovely palace, was having a wonderful party.

Mother: A party!

Stepsister 1: I will have a new dress!

Stepsister 2: I will have one, too.

Cinderella: I would like to go, too.

Mother: You?

Stepsister 1: You can't go!

Stepsister 2: You have to do the chores.

Narrator: Cinderella should probably have spoken up, but she knew that she would not get to go. And indeed, when the night of the prince's party arrived, Cinderella was given the hardest job of all—cleaning the chimney.

Mother: It is time to go.

Stepsister 1: I will be the most beautiful.

Stepsister 2: I will be the most charming.

Cinderella: And I will clean the chimney.

Narrator: Off the three went, party dresses glittering in the moonlight. Cinderella sadly watched them go, a tear running down through the dirt on her cheek.

Cinderella: A party would be fun.

Narrator: Suddenly Cinderella heard an unfamiliar voice behind her.

Fairy Godmother: You can go to the party.

Cinderella: Who are you?

Fairy Godmother: I am your fairy godmother.

Cinderella: You are?

Fairy Godmother: Do you want to go?

Cinderella: Oh, yes!

Fairy Godmother: Well then...

Narrator: The fairy waved her magic wand. Suddenly Cinderella was dressed in a beautiful gown complete with dainty crystal slippers fit for the prince's party.

Fairy Godmother: How is that?

Cinderella: It is beautiful!
But how will I get there?

Narrator: Waving her magic wand again, the fairy turned a ripe pumpkin into a coach and six mice into prancing horses.

Fairy Godmother: How is that?

Cinderella: Wonderful!

Fairy Godmother: You must promise me something.

Cinderella: What?

Fairy Godmother: You must be back by midnight.

Cinderella: I will.

Fairy Godmother: Then have a good time.

Cinderella: Thank you!

Narrator: The fairy vanished as Cinderella climbed into the beautiful carriage.

©1997 Good Apple

Cinderella: What fun!

Narrator: The prince's party was everything that Cinderella had imagined and more. From the instant she arrived, the prince would dance with no one else. In her new clothes, no one recognized her—not even her own family.

Mother: Who is that girl?

Stepsister 1: I don't know.

Stepsister 2: Me, either.

Narrator: Cinderella had such a wonderful time that she forgot to watch the clock. In the middle of a waltz, she realized what time it must be. As the clock began to chime, she ran toward her coach.

Prince: Where are you going?

Cinderella: I must go home!

Narrator: Cinderella reached the enchanted carriage just as it rounded a corner and changed back into a pumpkin. Her beautiful gown was gone too, and in its place were her old ragged clothes.

Cinderella: That was close!

Narrator: Cinderella realized that she had to walk home *and* with only one shoe, for she had lost the other one when she ran from the palace.

©1997 Good Apple

Cinderella: What a party!

Narrator: She made it home just before her mother and two stepsisters arrived.

Mother: We had fun!

Stepsister 1: There was good food.

Stepsister 2: There was lots of dancing.

Stepsister 1: The prince didn't dance with me.

Stepsister 2: Not with me, either.

Cinderella: Who then?

Mother: A beautiful stranger.

Narrator: That made Cinderella smile, and she went to bed that night happier than she'd ever been. It wasn't long before a messenger brought news that the prince was looking far and wide for the beautiful stranger.

Mother: Who could she be?

Stepsister 1: Could it be me?

Stepsister 2: Maybe it's me!

Narrator: Cinderella didn't reply—she was busy scrubbing the floor. She wondered how the prince would ever find the beautiful stranger. That night, Cinderella's fairy godmother visited her again.

©1997 Good Apple

Fairy Godmother: Cinderella.

Cinderella: Yes?

Fairy Godmother: He will find you.

Cinderella: Maybe. But he won't know me.

Fairy Godmother: Why?

Cinderella: I had a lovely dress.

Fairy Godmother: Yes.

Cinderella: Now I am dirty.

Fairy Godmother: Yes, but he has your slipper.

Cinderella: He does?

Fairy Godmother: Yes. He will find you.

Narrator: When Cinderella woke up the next morning, she couldn't be sure that the fairy godmother had really spoken to her or not. She went about her chores as usual.

Mother: Someone is coming.

Stepsister 1: Who is it?

Stepsister 2: It is the prince!

Narrator: Indeed it was! And in his royal hand was a crystal slipper. All of Cinderella's family ran into the yard to watch. The prince stopped at the first house.

Prince: Try this on.

Narrator: Of course, the shoe didn't fit, so the prince went on from house to house, asking for every lady to try the crystal slipper on. Finally he came to Cinderella's house.

Prince: Try this on.

Mother: Of course.

Narrator: The shoe did not fit. The mother's feet were far too big.

Prince: Try this on.

Stepsister 1: I will.

Narrator: The shoe did not fit. The first stepsister's big toe was too large.

Prince: Try this on.

Stepsister 2: It will fit.

Narrator: But the shoe did not fit. The second stepsister's foot was too wide. The prince looked at Cinderella, whose dress was dripping with soapy water from the floor and streaked with soot from the chimney.

Mother: Not her.

Prince: Why not?

©1997 Good Apple

Mother: She did not go.

Stepsister 1: She is too dirty.

Stepsister 2: She is too lazy.

Prince: She must try this on.

Narrator: The mother had almost convinced the prince that Cinderella could not possibly be the beautiful stranger he was looking for, when the fairy godmother appeared and gently tapped the prince with her magic wand.

Prince: Try this on.

Cinderella: All right.

Narrator: It was a perfect fit!

Prince: My new princess!

Cinderella: Me?

Prince: Yes.

Narrator: The fairy godmother instantly changed Cinderella into the beautiful stranger. She turned the mother and stepsisters into toads, for that was what they deserved for treating Cinderella so badly. There was a magnificent wedding—to which the three toads were *not* invited—and Cinderella and the prince lived happily ever after.

BIBLIOGRAPHY

Garner, Alan. *Jack and the Beanstalk.* Doubleday Books for Young Readers, 1992.

Kellogg, Steven. *Jack and the Beanstalk.* Morrow Junior Books, 1991.

North, Carol. *Jack and the Beanstalk.* Golden Press, 1982.

Brett, Jan. *Goldilocks and the Three Bears.* Dodd, Mead, 1987.

Marshall, James. *Goldilocks and the Three Bears.* Dial Books for Young Readers, 1988.

Petach, Heidi. *Goldilocks and the Three Bears.* Putnam & Grosset, 1995.

Ziefert, Harriet. *Goldilocks and the Three Bears.* Tambourine Books, 1994.

Galdone, Paul. *The Little Red Hen.* Ticknor & Fields, 1973.

Zemach, Margot. *The Little Red Hen: An Old Story.* Farrar, Straus & Giroux, 1983.

Ziefert, Harriet. *The Little Red Hen.* Viking, 1995.

Bell, Sally Claster. *The Gingerbread Man.* Western Publishing Company, 1990.

Kimmel, Eric A. *The Gingerbread Man.* Holiday House, 1993.

Schmidt, Karen Lee. *The Gingerbread Man.* Scholastic, 1985.

Galdone, Paul. *The Three Little Pigs.* Seabury Press, 1970.

Hillert, Margaret. *The Three Little Pigs.* Modern Curriculum Press, 1963.

Scieszka, Jon. *The True Story of the Three Little Pigs!* Viking Kestrel, 1989.

Ziefert, Harriet. *The Three Little Pigs.* Viking, 1995.

Brown, Margaret Wise. *Little Chicken.* Harper, 1971.

Hobson, Sally. *Chicken Little.* Simon & Schuster Books for Young Readers, 1994.

Kellogg, Steven. *Chicken Little.* William Morrow, 1989.

Dewan, Ted. *Three Billy Goats Gruff... or Three Strikes, Yer Out!* Scholastic, 1994.

Galdone, Paul. *Three Billy Goats Gruff.* Houghton Mifflin, 1973.

Rounds, Glen. *The Three Billy Goats Gruff.* Holiday House, 1993.

Ziefert, Harriet. *The Three Billy Goats Gruff.* Tambourine Books, 1994.

Marshall, James. *Hansel and Gretel.* Dial Books for Young Readers, 1990.

North, Carol. *Hansel and Gretel.* Western Publishing Company, 1990.

Ross, Tony. *Hansel and Gretel.* Overlook Press, 1994.

Easton, Samantha. *The Bremen Town Musicians.* Andrews & McMeel, 1991.

Plums, Ilse. *The Bremen Town Musicians.* Doubleday, 1980.

Stevens, Janet. *The Bremen Town Musicians.* Holiday House, 1992.

Galdone, Paul. *Little Red Riding Hood.* McGraw-Hill, 1974.
Marshall, James. *Red Riding Hood.* Dial Books for Young
    Readers, 1987.
Young, Ed. *Lon Po Po: A Red-Riding Hood Story From
    China.* Philomel Books, 1989.

Galdone, Paul. *Cinderella.* McGraw-Hill, 1978.
Hogrogian, Nonny. *Cinderella.* Greenwillow Books, 1981.
Martin, Rafe. *The Rough-Faced Girl.* Scholastic, 1992.
Perrault, Charles. *Cinderella or the Little Glass Slipper.*
    H. Z. Walck, 1971.